The

SELF-LOVE
BIBLE

How I Learned to Love Myself

Cici.B

THE CRIMSON KISS

*Dedicated to all of the women
who are on their self-love journeys.*

Be proud of yourselves.

To the man that I've had the most toxic relationship with and have since left behind, I am now... unrecognizable.

Word gets back to me that he often keeps up with my life from a distance via social media, and says things like, "That's not the real her." And, "She's not as bold as she wants people to believe she is."

The thing is... he is absolutely right.

The woman I am now is not who he remembers at all.

With him, I was underdeveloped. Broken. Unsure. I was lacking in the departments of self-love and confidence, which sent me on a search for love in all the wrong places. Ironically, this search also led me with a desperate need to be validated and accepted by the man in my life that I looked up to... him.

But see, he knew all of those things about me already, which is why he enjoyed me as much as he did.

I was the woman who fed both his ego, and his burning desire to have total control over another person. I was the one who never said no to him, never put any boundaries in place for him, or myself. I was the one who would drop any and everything for him, the

• • •

one who willingly put my life on hold and waited for him. No matter the hurtful things he said or did, I was the one who always forgave, and let him right back in... which is why he continued to say and do the things that he did. What a toxic cycle, indeed.

That said, I think it's important to understand that I'm not putting all the blame on him. If you really look at it, we both failed each other miserably. I taught him to treat me like I was less than because I'd already grown used to accepting that treatment from myself, and on his end, well... he took full advantage of it.
We were both fucked up in our own ways. Both battling and struggling with things internally. However, here's what lets me know that he's still fucked up:

He looks at me, now, and thinks, "That's not the real her," because the idea that I have grown and changed for the better—fixed my broken pieces, found my voice and confidence, learned how to love and take care of myself, thus, no longer needing validation or acceptance from anyone else— has never crossed his mind. Why? Simply put, he is the exact same person he was the day I mustered up some courage and decided it was time to leave both him, and that old version of myself, behind.

He has yet to evolve in his own mind, spirit, heart and soul, therefore, has no clue as to what evolution looks like in others. This is why I'm not mad at him. How can I be?

I had to let go of him, and all of the other toxic people who I was surrounded by in order to find me.
Perhaps, amongst other things he needs to do for himself, he has to let go of the woman I was when I was with him, in order to see the woman I've become without him.

Since beginning my author journey on Instagram, writing about the ups, downs and everything in between when it comes to my life and *past* relationships, two questions that I get asked quite often are: *"How did you learn to love yourself?"* and, *"After everything you've been though with toxic men, how do you manage your dating life now?"* The thing is, the answer to the first question is not a simple one. There are many layers to this self-love stuff; well, at least there are for me.

The answer to the second question, though, that's a lot easier. Actually, everything becomes a lot easier once you love yourself… so I've learned.

Part 1:

How I Learned to Love Myself

Sankofa

"to go back and fetch"

We must go back to reclaim our past
so we can move forward,
and we can understand why and how
we came to be who we are today.

Broken Pieces

I think the hardest thing for me when it came to this self-love stuff was coming to terms with the fact that I had to go back in time, dig, and find the root of where shit went wrong. Finding the root meant that there were a lot of things and people that I could possibly end up seeing in a different light, including myself...

and that shit was *terrifying*.

It meant that there were men in my past that I had once loved, then hated, that I may have to forgive.
It meant that I would possibly have to confront the single, most important person in my life—my mother—question her, get upset at her and worse, have feelings of disappointment towards her that I would have to sort through.
It meant that I would have to look at my own behaviours and interactions with other people throughout the course of my life thus far, and possibly be smacked with the reality that as many times as I've called others "toxic"... I too could very well be toxic in my own way.

Finding *the root* meant that there was a good possibility that the only world I had known and lived in for so long could get flipped upside down, and that there would be no going back. Whatever came with it, I'd have to face, accept, and work though.

There came a point in my adulthood, after taking a good look at myself and the extremely toxic relationships I constantly found myself in, that I said, "*Enough is enough*". I had a choice to make:

Continue living the way I was—including a never-ending fucking cycle of heartbreaks and mayhem—or go find the root of why I was the way that I was, allowed the things I allowed and kept going back to things and people who hurt me.

I knew that I could never change the past—what happened, happened—but I could definitely change the direction in which my future was headed.

My First Root:

Daddy *and* Mommy Issues

I remember being a kid
looking in the mirror at my face,
wondering if it looked liked yours at all.
I remember growing up and wondering
how tall you were, because compared to
everyone on my mother's side,
I was pretty damn small.

I remember staring at the color of my skin
wondering if we shared the same
complexion,
I remember wishing you were around
to teach me about the history
behind the color of my skin,
and guide me in the right directions.

I remember looking at my hair
and wondering if yours was thick
with tight curls too,
or did I have some aunties on your side
with hair like mine
who could teach me how to take care of it;
show me what to do.

I remember hating you for not being around,
but loving you at the same time…
and I didn't even know you.

*I remember the first time they called me
a nigger…
I was six years old and didn't even know
what the word meant,
but sitting on that school bus
on my way home,
I knew it was bad based on the way the older
kids chanted it in my direction,
and laughed until they were spent.*

*Every day on that bus
those same kids would tell me to sit my
"black ass" in the back.
I didn't understand it then,
but what could I do?
I was fucking six years old, shy,
outnumbered and scared.
So, I did what I was told…
I took my black ass to the back.*

*I didn't tell mom
because I didn't know how,
and she was already dealing with so much
shit from my stepdad, that my six-year-old
self thought it would only be an extra burden
on her shoulders, somehow.
She found out a year later though, one day
as I was getting off of the bus.
She was at the bottom of the driveway
waiting for me,*

and I guess that was the day that I'd had enough.

I got off that bus in tears, ran to her, and she held me tight.
"Baby girl, what's the matter?" She asked me, softly, but panicked at the same time as I sobbed in her arms, holding onto her for dear life.
I mustered up some courage, lifted my head and looked in her eyes,
"Mommy? What's a nigger?" I asked,
"And why am I black but you're white?"

...

About three years ago, I wrote the letter you just read to my biological father whom, till this day, I have never actually formally met. I've been writing him letters/poetry since I was a kid. Call it a form of self-therapy, if you will, because they were letters I would never send to him even if I wanted to. How could I? I didn't even know who he was.
I ended up finding my father's family (my grandfather and uncle) when I was thirty-one years old. As I pen this book, I am thirty-three.
It turns out that when the crack epidemic hit the black community in Montreal, in the 80's, both my father *and* uncle fell victim to that shit and have been addicted ever since.

My mother, who is part Italian and part French (Quebecois), had me when she was seventeen and was banned by her own father from the Italian side of the family for having a black baby. Because of this, I only grew up knowing my grandmother (my mother's, mother) and my two uncles (my mother's brothers).
There is an insane amount of controversy that surrounds the stories that I've been told my entire life about what down between my father and my mother before I was born (and why I never laid eyes on him), by both her, and her friends whom I began to question as

I got older. Out of respect for my mother,
due to the nature and severity of this
controversy, I've chosen not to disclose
these particular stories, in this story.

I spent my entire life wondering about my
father, though. Daydreaming about him.
Imagining how things could have been if he
and my mother were together in a loving,
healthy relationship. Imagining how things
could have been if they weren't together, but
he was there for me.
I also spent my entire life telling myself that
I didn't need him—which was a lie.
Did I survive without him? Of course.
But as I looked back on my life, I realized
that I absolutely needed my real father.

As you can probably gather from the poem I
wrote to him, I struggled a lot with the
colour of my skin as a child.
As much as I know my mother has always
loved me, she was unable to teach me how
to survive and be a woman of colour in this
world. She could she never prepare me for
all of the real-life shit I'd have to experience
as a woman of colour, nor could she ever
relate to these experiences.
I am not shitting on my mother here, by the
way. As a matter of fact, because I will be
speaking about my mother a lot throughout

this book, allow me to get this preface out of the way:

My mother is my whole damn world and my actual best friend. She raised me to the best of her capability, supported me throughout every single one of my highs and lows, and has *always* showed up for me. The things about my mother that I will be addressing, that had a negative impact on me growing up is *not* to shit on her. All I'm doing here is speaking the facts; and one of these facts is that my mother was not equipped with the tools to teach me how to navigate this world as **a woman of colour**, and because of this, not only did I begin to resent the man who I had never met for not being around to be a male role model for me, but also because he was not there to teach me about my black history as a young child.

...

When I was about three years old, my mother met and fell in love with a white man. When I was five, my younger brother was born. He had milky white skin, bright blonde hair and hazel eyes. When I turned seven, my other brother was born. Same white skin and blonde hair, but his eyes were a piercing bright blue. Then there was me—deep caramel coloured skin, thick, coily, dark brown hair and brown eyes.

Between the age of five to nine years old, we lived outside of the city of Montreal, on the countryside, where there were ZERO people of colour, and I do mean *none*. Everywhere we went people thought I was adopted. Every family picture we took I would stare at and feel so out of place. One of my brothers actually referred to me as "caca" when he began learning how to speak, because to him, never having laid eyes on another person of colour, that's what I resembled—*the shit that came out of his ass*.

I remember my mother flipping the actual fuck out the first time she heard him say it, and correcting him over and over again for months until he finally stopped. You may be asking yourself why it took so damn long for it to stop. Well, that's because while my mother was on one end with a straight face saying, "No. It's, CICI," my step-dad was on the other end laughing his ass off every time my brother would say it, thus *encouraging it*.

Don't worry, I'll get into my step-dad in a moment.

There is a running joke amongst my brothers and I that I am my mother's favourite child; but that joke stems from them watching our dynamic as we grew up. I think she always knew I felt out of place, like the black sheep (full pun intended), so she wanted to protect me as much as she could and make sure I knew that I was loved by her as much as she could. Let's face it: Not only did my brothers have two parents, they had two parents who they could easily see themselves in. I, on the other hand, had only one, and while I did see many of my own facial features and mannerisms in my mother...

she wasn't the same colour as me.

I would love to say that my brother's father always did his best to include me as his own child, but that would be a flat out lie. From what I have been told, he did in the beginning when he and my mother first met, and for a little while after my first brother was born, but I was too young to remember that part.

My earliest memories of him begin about a year *after* my first brother was born and, from what I remember, I never felt like he loved me at all. I felt like he only tolerated me.

I remember trying to call him, "Dad" at some point when I was extra young, but it was only because my brother was calling him that and I wanted to feel included. That shit didn't last long though. I felt awkward saying it, and he looked like he felt just as awkward hearing me say it.
(By the way, my mother never once asked me to call him, Dad. I did it on my own.)

My step-dad, who was a few years older than my mother, had a lot of money and was a powerful man. My mother had always been independent, but after my first brother was born, my step-dad managed to talk her into being a stay at home mom. The house that we lived in, on the countryside, was actually a mini mansion that he'd had built. Cathedral ceilings, enormous kitchen and separate dining room, bathrooms complete with Jacuzzis, and a huge mezzanine that overlooked the main floor/living room.

The house sat isolated amidst acres of land, which he also owned. In the back of our house you could find the pool, on the right side of the house you could find a stable which housed our two horses, Polko and Argyle, and standing on guard at the front of our house you could find my besties, our two King Germans Shepherds, Trixi and Brutis.

I *looooved* our animals so much. I'd play in the front yard with my dogs all day long, while running in the house every so often to bug my mom about riding Argyle. I have some amazing memories of my mother and I riding Argyle together, he was my favorite because he was calm, gentle and always happy to see me. Polko, on the other hand, was wild, stubborn as fuck, and the only person who could ever get near him or ride him was my mother—I learned that lesson after he basically snuffed my little ass for getting too close to him while my mother's back was turned. I was like, "Okay! Well forget you too then! Rude." Never bothered him again.

It wasn't too long after my mother became a certified stay at home mom that my step-dad became a full-blown alcoholic and avid user of cocaine... and that's when shit got real.

He began yelling at my mother for the most ridiculous of things.

If his meal wasn't at the correct temperature of warmth when he got home, she'd get yelled at and called a slew of vulgar names. If his shirts weren't ironed to his liking, the same thing.
There were times when he would come home drunk and high late at night after everyone was already in bed, flip on all of the lights, wake my mother out of her sleep and yell at her for missing a spot while washing the windows.
The first few times I ever heard him yell at her from upstairs in my bedroom, my young mind didn't understand why he was yelling at her, and why she wasn't yelling back at him. As time went on, of course he got bolder, and began doing that shit right in front of us kids, and it was only then that I understood.

One night he had come home in time for dinner.
I helped set the table, made sure my little brother was secure in his high-chair and had his favorite toy with him, then sat as my mother began sharing out the plates.
Something about her energy was odd, and I sensed that shit, immediately. Normally,

when it was just us getting ready for dinner, we would sing a song at the same time, or dance around being silly; but this time she was eerily quiet. I followed her lead and I too remained quiet.

Once all of the food was shared, I began to eat as did my step-dad. I will never forget this moment, ever. Out of nowhere, he suddenly and violently spit his food back in his plate and looked over at my mother who hadn't even sat down yet. "Why the fuck is this cold?" He barked at her, and I jumped in my seat. With my own food in my in my mouth, I remember thinking to myself, *it's not even cold though.*

I peered over at my mother and that's when I saw it—fear had washed over her face and leaked through her eyes. I had never seen my mother look like that, ever, and seeing her scared, scared me.

"It just came off of the stove," she replied, softly.

"So, you're calling me a fucking liar?" My step-dad challenged.

I couldn't believe my ears.
She didn't call you a liar, I thought to myself. *She's telling you that food is straight off of the stove.*

"No, I'm not calling you a liar," She
answered in an even softer tone than before.
"I can heat it up further for you if…"
"You know what?" He bellowed, cutting her
off. "You're a real fucking piece of work."
He aggressively pushed his plate towards the
middle of the table, and stood, "I'm out
working all day, dealing with everything I
have to deal with, and THIS is what I have
to come home to? A woman who can't even
make sure my meal is hot? You're pathetic.
Clean this shit up, I'm going out."

I was fucking stunned. He walked out of the
dining room and out of the house, slamming
the door behind him, and I jumped at the
sound and my brother started crying in his
chair. Instinctively, I turned my attention
towards him, picked up his toy and began
waving it around in front of him while I
sang, "Twinkle, twinkle little star…" He
started smiling as he reached for it.
I glanced over at my mother who was
clearing my step-dads plate, and studied her.
I could tell that she wanted to cry but was
trying to keep a brave face. I whispered to
her, "Mommy, the food isn't cold. It's really
good and warm." She looked up at me, burst
into tears, walked over to me and hugged me
tightly.

• • •

This would be the beginning of me watching my mother be verbally, then physically abused, and exactly where I would begin to battle with feelings of disappointment towards her, hatred for my step-dad, and even more resentment for the father I never had.

Over the next couple of years, my step-dad got worse. I'd often awake to the sounds of him either hitting her, or yelling at her. Then, like clockwork, after he'd tire from abusing my mother in whichever way he saw fit for that night and pass out, she'd run upstairs, grab my brothers and I, a change of clothes for us, then pile us into her car. We'd either go to a cheap hotel for a few nights, or we'd drive a couple of hours to the city and stay with a friend of my moms. Things got so bad, in fact, that she began leaving bags full of clothes for all of us, diapers, jars of baby food and snacks for my brothers in the trunk of her car. She also had to start taking the dogs with us on our mad dashes because my step-dad would awake at some point, realize she had left, and take his anger out on them. How did we know this? One time we came home and found Brutis badly beaten in the front yard—that's how.

I had grown so accustomed to these late-night escapes, that the moment I heard yelling downstairs, I'd get out of my bed, take my little brothers out of theirs, and get us ready to go.

I have always loved my mother more than anything in this world, and at a very young age I already understood that she was all I had. But, I was extremely confused about many other things and, admittedly, this confusion developed into me having many angry moments:

Why was she staying with him when he hurt her this way?

Why did she let him talk to her like that?

Why didn't she call the police?

Why didn't we move away from him?

*Why did she still clean and cook, iron his clothes, do **anything** for him?*

I'm a grown woman now, and having been through my own fair share of shit with men, I am aware of real-life things, like:
Mental and emotional manipulation and abuse. Superiority complexes. Narcissism. Alcoholism. Drug addiction. Gaslighting tactics. Etc.
But I was just a little girl when these things were taking place in front of my ears and eyes.

I had no concept of, "It's complicated."
To me, in my young mind, it was simple—
"Let's get outta here!"
How could I have known just how much of
a grasp he had on her? How strategic his
process was? How he purposely isolated my
mother over the years so she would feel like
she had no one but him? How the whole
reason why he had built that house on the
fucking countryside, in the middle of
fucking nowhere, was to aide in that
isolation? He knew that none of my mothers
friends or the family members she had left
would be able to make that trip up there to
visit regularly.

My mother had an intense love for horses
since she was a child. How could I have
known that the horses in the stable were
"gifts" to her after he had beaten the shit out
of her one day? How could I have known
that all of the bank accounts were in his
name and she had no money to leave?
How could I have known that by the time
things were out of control, my mother didn't
want to tell my grandmother or uncles what
was going on inside of our house because
she was embarrassed, ashamed… afraid?

… I couldn't. I couldn't possibly have
known all of that.

I was nine years old when, one day, my mother woke up, came into my room with some garbage bags and said, "Come on, baby girl. Take everything you love and put them in these bags. We're moving to a new home."
"Just us?" I asked, referring to just her, my brothers and I. She managed a smile, then offered a wink, "Just us, baby girl."

Little did I know that ever since the abuse began, whenever my step-dad left her money to do the groceries or buy us new clothes or toys, my mother had been carefully taking a dollar here, ten dollars there, and hiding it.

She had been quietly plotting our biggest escape yet, all along.

. . .

Once we moved back to the city (without my step-dad), of course life was better for us, immediately. My mother resumed the independence she'd had before him, and I watched her as she held down our fort.

She worked many jobs, simultaneously, in order to make ends meet, but still found a way to always have time for us *and* manage to make time for herself. Growing up, I always found that so incredibly amazing. I respected and admired her for her drive, determination, and overall hustle. Plus, I was so proud of her for finding a way to leave my step-dad. She was my actual hero. She was also (and still very much is) extremely classy and graceful. My mother had this way of making a ten-dollar outfit look like it was designer, and costume jewelry look like they were real gold and diamonds.

By the time I was twelve years old, my mother was only twenty-nine years old. When you really think about it, as she was watching me grow up, I was watching her grow up, too.

I always shake my head in amazement whenever I think about that. I couldn't imagine myself at twenty-nine years old with an almost teenage daughter. That shit is mind-blowing to me.

• • •

Saturday nights were when she would go out salsa dancing in the Latin clubs with her closest friends (who were mostly Dominican), and who my brothers and I would call our aunties. This is where I was introduced to Dominican culture and why I am so well versed and comfortable within it—I was surrounded by it.

She'd start getting ready around 9PM, salsa and merengue music played at a medium volume from her boombox, and I'd wander into her bedroom, fiddle with the perfumes on her dresser, spray some on me, then sit on her bed and watch as she blow-dried then flat ironed her dark blonde hair bone straight, then put on her makeup—which was very little may I add.

Mascara and eyeliner which accentuated her hazel eyes, a tad bit of foundation, and her signature lipstick: A medium brown lip-liner and a gold lipstick.

It was always after this that she'd usher me out of her room and close the door so she could dress, then open the door again, which was the signal that I could come back in. I'd pause by the doorway for a second, staring at her in awe. First things, first:

My mother stood at 5'9 with a pair of long, slender legs that seemed to never end. At the age of twenty-nine, she had the type of curves that many women today get surgery

to achieve. Her waist was small, and her tummy was as flat as a board. Her breasts, three whole kids later, still sat up plump and effortless on her chest. Her thighs were shapely, and thicker than any other white woman I had ever seen in my life at that time, and her booty... *listen...*
Again, it was the type of booty that so many women, today, go under the knife to get.

She was never a flashy dresser. Solid, and mostly dark colours were her thing. Lot's of blacks, navy blues, dark greys and every now and then, a dash of white or beige. My mom had a rule of thumb when it came to dressing, she always said, "Never sacrifice grace and class for cheap attention. If you're going to wear a skirt that is above your knees, then wear a shirt that doesn't show any cleavage. If you're going to wear a dress, pick one that flatters your body-shape. Always pick materials that hug your body just enough, but aren't slinky and cheap looking to the eye or touch. When it comes to jeans, you can *always* dress them up with the right pair of heels and shirt. And when it comes to colours, you can never go wrong with an all black outfit—black is timeless, elegant, and even if your entire outfit was twenty-five dollars, with the right accessories, heels and posture, you can walk into a room looking like you just got off of a private jet."

Till this very day, I adhere to the majority of those very things. Not because I have to, and not that I haven't experimented outside of them on my own, but simply because I always loved my mothers style and felt equally comfortable adopting it for myself.

"You're so beautiful, Mommy," I'd say, still leaning against the doorframe.
She'd flip her hair over to the side, then smile at me, "Well, you look just like me, so guess what that means?" She'd ask, and I'd blush and shrug my shoulders, "Sometimes I look like you, but my nose is wider than yours. My eyes are brown and boring, and my hair... I hate my hair," I'd admit. "I want it to be straight like yours."

We literally went through this at least once a week; I shit you not.

My mom would stop what she was doing, come over to me and say, "Baby girl... how many times do I have to tell you that your hair is absolutely gorgeous? I, and so many others would kill to have hair like yours!"
"Yeah, right," I'd answer, unconvinced.
"Cici... you are beautiful. Your hair is full

of life. Your brown eyes are not boring—
they are deep and mysterious—and your
nose is the cutest nose in the world; it fits
the shape of your face, perfectly. Everything
about you, and what comes with you, is
what makes you who you are. Always
remember that. I love you."

I'd offer her a smile in return for the words
that I knew came straight from her heart and
say, "I love you too, Mommy," but deep
down was a lingering question that would
end up haunting me well into my adult
years: *How can I know who I am when there
is an entire half of me that is missing?*

Remember when I said that as my mother
was watching me grow up, I was watching
her grow up, too?
A major part of me watching her grow up
was beginning to realize that she, like any
other woman, was longing for the love and
companionship from a man.
She'd had a few relationships after she
escaped from my step-dad, but most of them
were all toxic too. She never entertained,
dated, or got into a relationship with a white
man again though, and I must admit a huge
part of me really liked that. I guess, in
retrospect, I was so desperate for a black
man to teach me about my black roots, that

The Self-Love Bible

part of me thought that maybe one of her boyfriends would be "the one" for her, and we could all be a new family.

The irony of it all—here was my mother looking for love, and here was her daughter quietly hoping for a father figure in every man her mother brought home.

The move back to the city was not only exciting for me because we were getting away from the devil, but also because once we got there, people with the same skin colour as me, and darker, were in abundance. I didn't get anymore strange looks as I played outside in the front of our new duplex, and I didn't get ostracized at school. As a matter of fact, on my very first day of school registration in 1994, I met my very first city friends who, unbeknownst to me at the time, would end up being my crew (or "squad" for all the new school people) well into my adult years. They were two black girls—one about a shade darker than myself, and the other a soft mocha complexion.

I was standing in line with my mother and was holding my younger brother by the hand. The lighter girl of the two walked right up to me and said, "Hi. I'm Sade," then she pointed to the other girl who was off to the side, watching our exchange, "And that's my best friend, Samantha. Is that your kid?" Taken aback, I looked up at my mother who was laughing at the question, then looked back at Sade and blurted out, "Ew, no! I'm nine years old! This is my little brother. Gross."

She shrugged her shoulders then popped her gum, "I was just askin'... you look a lil' older and you never know. Anyways, you coming to this school this year? Where do you live? And what's your name?"

Again, I looked at my mother who was now smiling at Sade, clearly amused by her boldness, then I looked back at Sade and studied her for a second. I thought she was so pretty, standing there with her hand on her hip, her hair tied in a high bun secured with two pink and blue bobbles. *I wonder if she can show me how to do my hair like that too,* I thought to myself.

"Hello?" She questioned, impatiently, snapping me out of my thoughts.

"Huh? Oh. My name is Cici, I live on Orchard street and yes, I'm coming to this school this year."

She smiled wide and shrieked, "We live on that street, too!" then wrapped her arm in mine. "Let's walk home together, me you and Sam, and we'll introduce you to our other friends and we can be a crew!"

I looked at my mother one last time for confirmation, and she nodded her head in approval. "Okay!" I said, excitedly.

I was formally introduced to three other girls, and our crew ended up being a beautiful mix of all different shades with Caribbean blood—Jamaican, Trinidadian, and Bajan. We all lived on the same street, and as it turned out, most of our mothers had already known each other from back in their own high school days.
It wasn't too long before we all considered each other extended family, and us young girls became inseparable; and just like that, I finally felt some form of belonging.
Today, as I look back on my journey with my crew, I truly believe that God placed me there to give me all that I needed to learn, not only about my black history, but also my Jamaican culture, as I later discovered that my father was indeed, black Jamaican.

It only took a few months for my new friends and I to realize we had a lot more in common than we thought.
Like me, they were fatherless with young mothers who were looking for love just like mine was. We grew up watching our moms get into relationship after relationship, only for those relationships to turn toxic, them

stay and make excuses for those toxic relationships, then when those toxic relationships finally ended in the most dramatic ways, we would be the ones to console them.

None of us ever knew what a "healthy" relationship between a man and woman looked like because there weren't ever any examples of those around us. All we knew about relationships was arguing, yelling, physical and emotional abuse, and putting up with it all because that's all any of us ever saw. **To us, that shit was normal.** The thing is, now that I'm older, I've learned that many of our grandmothers were in abusive and toxic relationships as well. See how viciously history can repeat itself, and just how much of an impact what you do in front of your children *truly* has on them? **Our mothers didn't know what the fuck they were doing.** Like I said, they were all young women themselves, and they'd had children in their teenage years. **How could they teach us self-love when they didn't even know it for themselves? How could they teach us how to have healthy exchanges with men, when they didn't know how to have them?**

By the time some of our mothers got a grip on their own lives and realized that their relationships with men were actually toxic, it was too late. The damage to us young and impressionable little girls had already been done. **We were fucked**. A leader leads by example, and unfortunately, the example they accidently set for us by staying with men who treated them like actual shit is what we took with us, and ended up believing love was.

For most of my friends and I, our teenage years were when the cravings for a man in our lives really began to surface, and we subconsciously began searching for a father figure, a protector, acceptance and unconditional love in every high school boy we met. As much as I'd like to admit otherwise, this search for a father figure continued throughout the course of my adult life and only truly ended once I found out who my father was. That being said, you can see how easy it was for me to slip into what seemed to be a never-ending cycle of staying in toxic relationships with men, and also what kind of unfair pressure I put on these men due to the pedestal I placed them on; especially the boyfriends I had in my teens and very early twenties, who, when you really think about it, were actually only young boys, themselves.

• • •

My longing for acceptance and love from a man blurred the lines that separated right from wrong. In my mind, no matter how badly I was being treated, at least I had someone.

My Second Root:

Acceptance Issues

Being passive, broken, and timid with a desire for acceptance that was so overwhelmingly powerful, I became a people pleaser in public, but a rebel behind closed doors. I always had my own mind and my own strong opinions, the problem was, **I only allowed myself to embrace them when I was alone.**

Allow me to elaborate.

My newfound crew of coloured girls gave me a sense of belonging that I had never felt before, and I never wanted to jeopardize that—ever. So, I kept my mouth shut for the most part, agreed and went along with mostly everything my circle of friends said and did, especially, Sade. She was the ringleader of our crew, and the truth of the matter was…

she was a *fucking bully* and *we all knew it*.

From the beginning of our friendship, right through our teenage years and even well into our adulthood, Sade's behaviour only worsened, and we, as a crew, only continued to enable it by never standing up to her. Actually, most of us ended up just abiding by her "laws" and subscribing to her moods. If she had a problem with one girl in the

crew, then the rest of us had to have a problem with her, too. Considering where I was coming from, I really didn't want to give anyone a reason to have conflict with me and take the chance of being banned. Interestingly enough, though, Sade would stand up for us against outsiders—especially for me. If someone else in school had a problem with me, she would be the first one at my defence, speaking up for me (A.K.A cussing them out). It was as if no one else was allowed to shit on us *but her*. Know what I mean? It was okay when she was the one saying mean things, or belittling us, but it wasn't okay when anyone else did it.
I guess that's also part of the reason why we were all so loyal to her, because as kids, it looked like she always had our backs.
So you see, the blurred lines that separated right from wrong due to my longing for acceptance and love went way beyond the realm of men, and seeped into my friendships as well; which for me, represented a place where I could learn about my black roots and be comfortable in my skin. What a shitshow, huh?

Keeping my mouth shut all the time, being afraid to stand up for myself—and to the other girls for that matter—and tolerating massive amounts of what I know now to be abuse, basically made me both a doormat *and* an easy target. That was the dynamic when I was around my crew, but alone, I was totally different. Here's the thing: As much as I loved feeling like I had a sense of belonging (even if it was abusive as fuck), I also really loved doing my own thing, alone. I always had a sense of independence because at a very early age my mother instilled it in me. She also encouraged me to embrace what would turn out to be two extremely powerful tools in my life—*creativity* and *self-motivation*.

An example of my early independence is when I was learning how to tie my shoelaces. There's a home video that I recently came across, and in it, I was sitting on the side of my aunts balcony with my shoelaces untied. My aunt comes over, ties the laces on one shoe as I watch her carefully. When she goes to tie the laces on the other shoe, I put my little hand up to her and say, "No." She smiles, backs away, and lets me do it by myself. The video cuts after that, but I was told that I sat there for a good while trying to tie my own laces. My aunt tried to come back again to help me, and I refused. Eventually, I got it (to the best of my little abilities) and hopped up, proud of myself, and resumed playing in the yard.

When it comes to my creativity and self-motivation, my mother often tells stories of how I would wake up in the morning, get myself dressed, then play in my room or outside in the yard for hours all by myself. I would *always* find *something* to do. Whether it was colouring in my colouring books, playing with my dolls, or playing with our two dogs—I always found a way to create fun for myself. Once I learned how to read and write, well, that was the real topper. When my nose wasn't in a book, you could be sure to find me in my room writing my truest feelings out in a copybook, or creating a fictional piece (complete with characters, scenery and dialogue).

At heart, I was "a loner", and while I very much loved it, I craved a balance and was struggling with finding that. I wanted to know that I could slip away and be with myself and my imagination, but that I could also still have my spot, if you will, amongst my peers when I wanted to be around people. I was an ambivert. Something I only learned and *truly* embraced about myself a few years ago. **I can be social if the occasion calls for it**, and enjoy it, but not every day and not all the time. The same way **I can be alone** and enjoy it, but not all 365 days out of the year.

The concept of introvert, ambivert and extrovert isn't something that is taught to teens (perhaps it is now, but back when I was in high school, it definitely was not), so no one understood shit like:

Personal space. Needing to recharge. Loving your friends but not wanting to be around them some days and it having nothing to do with them. Social butterflies. Spotlight lovers. Non-lovers of the spotlight but it somehow always gravitating towards them. Natural charm. Natural ambition. Independence. Codependency.

We didn't know what any of that shit meant, or was for that matter—so how could we respect any of it?

As I got a little further into my high school years, probably around the age of fourteen, the emotional burden of everything began to take its toll on me and I started rebelling, but in very subtle ways.
I would cut class a few times a week, which I knew would result in me getting grounded by mother, and that's exactly what I wanted. In my teenage mind, what better way to have some alone time without being questioned by my friends than getting grounded? I'd also start purposely getting to

school late just so that I didn't have to deal
with my friends first thing in the morning
and so that I could get a detention for being
late just so I wouldn't have to deal with
them after school, either.

Though my mother and I had a very close
bond and she was the type of mother that I
could talk to about anything, there were
some things and feelings that I just didn't
know how to make sense of for myself back
then, let alone explain to her or anyone else.

My Third Root:

Abusive Men

"You like broken, naive women who have yet to find their own voices are still searching for their place in this world," I seethed at him. "You like them because it's easier to manipulate them into believing that your voice is the only one that matters, and that their place in this world is behind you, abiding by your rules."

"B, ju-just calm down for a se…"

"SHUT UP!" I yelled, suddenly, pointing the piece of the broken mirror I held in my hand towards him, "I AM DONE WITH YOU TELLING ME WHAT TO DO."
He raised his hands in the air, as if to surrender, and slowly took a few steps back backwards. Tears streamed down my face as I fixated on him, "What are you backing up for? You scared?" Silence. "ANSWER MY FUCKING QUESTION YOU INSECURE, NAPOLEON COMPLEX HAVING PIECE OF SHIT."

"Y-e-yes. Yes!" He managed. "You're scaring me, okay?"
I smiled the way only a mad woman does. "Interesting. The back of my head is bleeding because you shoved me into the mirror, all because you got angry with me

FOR NOT LISTENING TO YOU
BECAUSE I WAS CALLING ANGEL TO
ASK HER THE NAME OF A FUCKING
RESTAURANT THAT YOUR BITCH ASS
WANTED TO GO TO, and now… *you're*
scared? That's really fucking interesting."
I took a deep breath and shook my head.
"Well, looks like this broken and naive
woman finally found her voice," I looked
down at the glass in my hand, "And a
weapon. Get the fuck out of my house," I
ordered. "B, I'm sorry! It was an accident! I
was ju…"

"AN ACCIDENT? YOU'RE SORRY?
JUST LIKE SIX MONTHS AGO WHEN
YOU CHOKED ME UNCONSCIOUS
AND HAD TO LITERALLY GIVE ME
MOUTH TO MOUTH RESUSCITATION?
You said that was an accident, too, and you
were sorry then, too. Nah. NO. GET THE
FUCK OUT OF MY HOUSE BEFORE
I…" There was a knock at the front door,
and I heard the panicked voice of my girl,
Angel, on the other side of it, "B? B! Are
you okay?" She pounded on the door,
furiously. "NIGGA, PUT YOUR HANDS
ON HER AGAIN AND SEE IF I DON'T
FUCKING KILL YOU." More pounding.
"B! PLEASE, OH MY GOD. PLEASE
OPEN THE DOOR."

I think I had been having an out-of-body experience the whole time because hearing Angel's voice seemed to bring me back into the room... back into myself.
Though I was extremely relieved that she was there, I wondered how she had known. Immediately, I remembered that my piece of shit boyfriend had attacked me right after I said the words, "Alright, girl. Thanks. Talk to you later." I guess I never pressed the "end" button, and neither did Angel.

My eyes still locked on him, I backed up towards the door and opened it.
A bare-faced Angel dressed in black sweatpants, a black oversized hoodie and black sneakers bolted past me, ready to attack, and I immediately dropped the piece of glass that was in my hand and ran after her. I caught her by her sweater right before her fist connected with my completely caught off guard, boyfriends face.

"NO, B. FUCK THIS NIGGA, LEMME GO!"
"ANGEL, STOP. STOP!" I yelled as I fought to restrain her.
Though I absolutely wanted him to get fucked up, I was thinking about my friend first. I did not want her to get herself into

any sort of trouble, or get hurt in the act of trying to defend me.

The piece of shit slithered his way by us, and without another word, ran out the front door that was still open.
"B!" Angel yelled at me as we remained locked in our struggle. She was crying, and those tears didn't mean that she was sad— they meant that she was in full-fledged beast mode.

After what seemed to be forever of wrestling with her, finally, she calmed down a bit and wrapped her arms around me, hugging me tightly. The hug signaled my body that I was safe, and forced every single emotion that I was feeling out of me through a flood of tears. In the arms of one of my truest friends, I cried, and I cried, and I cried some more. This was the second man to put his hands on me, and I vowed to God, that he would be the last.

. . .

Like all of my relationships, that one started out with a man who swept me off my feet, but also a fuckton of bright red flags that I ignored. He showed signs of control issues from the jump. Made little "jokes" about things that I liked about myself that he wanted me to change. Told me that every single one of my friends were jealous of our relationship, which, in hindsight, was his way of trying to isolate me so that I would have no one but him... just like my step-dad did to my mom.

Why did I ignore the bright red flags?

Because my longing for love and validation from a man trumped the fuck out of them—that's why.

I think back to that day in my house, and how differently everything could have played out.

What if he would have smashed my head so hard against the mirror, that it killed me? What if Angel had hung up the phone before she had the chance to hear the fight and my screams? What if she would have gotten there too late? What if I wasn't able to grab her quick enough and *she* killed him out of pure rage and in my defence? What if I had used the piece of glass that was in my hand on him that day?

• • •

Scary as fuck.

Not all of my toxic relationships resulted in physical abuse, but all of them had different forms of abuse, nonetheless.
Like my mother, I was attracted to powerful men, or, what I *thought* "powerful" was, and they were attracted to me. In my eyes, being "powerful" and being "a protector" were one and the same. What I didn't realize was that these "powerful" men we're merely little boys playing dress up, and came with an array of complexes and deep, dark insecurities of their own. Sure, the package they came in was always shiny, smooth, dapper and debonair. Polished, strong and secure on the outside. Rusted, weak and insecure as fuck on the inside.

Now, here's where shit got even realer:

If I removed each of their preferred weapons of abuse from the equation and got completely honest with myself, which I did...

looking at them was merely looking at a reflection of myself.

My Fourth Root:

Anger Issues

For a very long time I harboured a lot of anger towards the men I ended up in toxic relationships with. I hated them all, literally. To me, they were fucking scum for all the shit they had put me through, from cheating, to abuse, to real-life trauma.

I also harboured an equal amount of hate for my step-dad for what he had put my mom through. But, it wasn't until I started digging to find my own roots, that I ended up taking a moment to consider the roots of every toxic man I had ever known.

Now, admittedly, this was hella hard for me to do, and I stress the words, ***hella hard,*** to the top of the high heavens. We all have a level of pride in us that bears its teeth when we've been done wrong and hurt.

"Consider those pieces of shit, for what?" My pride snarled. *"Fuck them. They don't deserve consideration. Did they ever consider you while they were treating **you** like shit? Did your step-dad ever consider your mother while he was beating **her** ass? I think the fuck not."*

Here's what I've learned about this type of pride though: **It holds you hostage to hypocrisy.**

To add to the pride, as I slowly began to open up to a few people around me about what I had been considering, I was met with this sentence: *"Stop making excuses for the men who treated you like fucking shit."*

But, was I truly making excuses for them? Or was I simply coming to a point in my life where I was able to come to terms with *their reasons*, because I was beginning to come to terms with my own?

Listen, I would *never* take any of the toxic men I was with back, and if my mother ever thought about taking my step-dad back, I'd for sure lose my whole entire shit—let's be 5000% clear on that. All I'm saying here is, if I was able to realize that I was the way *I* was with men due to *my* childhood, why could those men not be the way *they* were with women due to *theirs*?

Perspective. Context. Understanding. Empathy.

I would be lying through my front teeth if I were to say that it didn't take damn near everything in me to push my pride and hatred to the side, allow myself to think back to the stories of those men, and remember the broken homes they too came from; some far worse broken than my own,

and that you would think only existed in a
persons worst nightmares.

Equipped with this knowledge, I had to ask
myself: *How could I possibly go on hating
these men?*

I'm **not saying** that any of them **were right**
for the shit that they did. What I am offering
is just the reality of shit, which is:

I was a direct product of my environment,
and so were they. I didn't know what a
healthy relationship between a man and a
woman looked like, and neither did they.

I didn't understand the importance of self-
love or how to practice it, and neither did
they. I had never seen my mother be
properly loved by a man, and they had never
seen a man properly love their mother.

I thought abusive relationships were normal;
and guess what?

So. Did. They.

No matter how "mature we all were for our
age", as many of our elders so often told us,
it didn't trump *who* and *what* we all really
were on the inside:

**Just a bunch of broken ass little girls and
boys who had no clue what the fuck we
were doing, or of the long-term**

● ● ●

**consequences of our actions and
behaviours.**

Whether or not my step-dad and the boys
from my past that I referred to as "men"
went on their own self-love journeys, or got
some much-needed therapy at some point
during their lives was, and still is, *none of
my business*. All I knew was that I could no
longer hold onto these negative feelings,
thoughts, and overall hatred for them. It was
time to forgive them in my heart, and mean
it, so that I could set myself free from all of
the negativity that had been weighing me
down for so long, and ultimately preventing
me from being the best version of myself
and living my best life.

The Silver Lining:
Knowledge is Power

The day I found out who my real father was, I was given a phone number to his childhood home by a woman who I always refer to as my mentor; very well known within the black community here, in Montreal, and only a couple of years younger than my mother, she was one of the people who helped me with my search. Turned out that my grandfather (his father) still lived in that home.

With trembling hands, I took one of the deepest breaths I have probably ever taken in my *entire* life, and dialed the number I had scribbled onto the paper. An elderly man with a slight Jamaican accent answered on the third ring, "Yes, hello?"… and a part of me—the scared part of me—wanted to hang up the phone.

Fuck it, no turning back.

"Um… H-Hi," I stammered, "Is this___?" (I said his full name). "Yes it is; and whom would be asking?" *Come on, just spit it out,* I urged myself. "Um… Okay, so my name is Cici, and this is going to sound pretty crazy, but…" I paused, shaking my head thinking of how off-putting what I was about to say would probably be to this man, then soldiered on, "I think that ___ is my father, and that you're my grandfather."

There was complete silence from the other end, and I squeezed my eyes shut as I felt an enormous lump forming in my throat. After what seemed like an eternity of silence, but in all actuality was only about thirty seconds, he replied, "Well… Come down to the house. Let me get a proper look at you."

My palms were sweating.
My palms *never* sweat.

I wiped them on the sides of my jeans, jotted down his address and told him I was on my way. A half an hour later I was on his front porch, ringing the doorbell.
I had no idea what to expect, and it was only in that moment that I realized that my whole body was shaking. I heard the unlocking of the door from the other side, and I took another deep breath.
The door opened, and standing in front of me was an elderly man with a rich caramel complexion, and an astonishing pair of sea blue eyes (which, completely caught me off guard) that lit up as he peered back at me.
He smiled, warmly, "Well then, no need for you to *think* you may be my granddaughter

when I know for a fact that you are. You look exactly like my wife."

I immediately burst into a fit of tears, and he reached his hand out for me and gently said, "Come, come. It's okay. Everything is going to be okay."

He guided me into the house, then into the living room. Everything was still very 90's looking, from the flower print sofas to the wall-units and bookshelves, but all was immaculately clean and not an item was out of place. It was as if no one ever went in there. My eyes traveled through the room, soaking everything in, and suddenly... my heart stopped.

There, on the wall, was a blown-up picture of a young man, grinning slightly, with skin the same colour as mine and cheekbones as high as mine. I stared into his familiar deep, brown, mysterious eyes. Familiar, because those were the eyes that had been staring back at me through every mirror I have ever looked into.

A few tears slid down my cheeks.
It was him.

I turned towards my grandfather for confirmation and he nodded his head, almost

as if he had read my thoughts, "Yes. That is
him. May,1984."
I focused my attention back to the picture as
I wiped the flow of tears from my cheeks.
Finally, I was face to face with the man I
had been imagining my entire life.
"Hi, dad…" I whispered.

I spent the rest of the afternoon with my
new-found grandfather as he took me on a
tour of the house, spoke about my father,
uncle and grandmother, my Jamaican
heritage, exactly where he and my
grandmother were born and raised
(Mandeville, Jamaica) and how they
migrated to Canada. He pulled out every
photo album he owned for me, and we sat
around his kitchen table going through every
single photo, one by one, as he told me the
backstory for each. He also let me know that
he still had a house in Mandeville and
always spent a few months out of the year
over there.
He talked about his own family tree and
revealed that one of his grandparents was
white (Irish white, to be exact), which
explained where he had inherited his blue
eyes from.

It's crazy how many feelings I had that day;
I was overwhelmed, sad, happy, upset, hurt

and relieved all at the same time, but there was one feeling in particular that overrode them all—gratitude.

I was so incredibly grateful for that day, and for my grandfather making it happen for me. Let's be honest—he *didn't* have to. He could have hung on me when I had called. He could have decided not to let me in when I showed up. He could have been a mean old man. He could have laughed in my face and told me I was crazy… but he didn't. Instead, he welcomed me into his home and showed me exactly who the other half of me was.

I learned that, unfortunately, my grandmother (his wife) passed away five years prior, and I wanted to kick myself for not having gone on this search sooner. But when I looked at her pictures, the most incredible wave of comfort washed over me. He was right—I looked *exactly* like her. I saw where both my dad and I got our high cheekbones from, and to my surprise, she had the same dimple in her left cheek when she smiled, as I did in mine when I smiled. Water in my eyes, I smoothed my fingers over a photo of her in her younger days. She was standing in her living room, wearing dark brown bell bottoms with a checkered beige and brown blouse. Her hair was out in a big fro, and she was smiling confidently

with one hand on her hip, flirting with the camera. "Is it okay if I have this one?" I asked my grandfather. He gazed at the picture and smiled, as if he were reminiscing to himself, then nodded his head, yes.
He also let me keep a few pictures of my dad, and the entire family.

As we spoke about my dad, he never did say that he was on drugs, exactly. Instead, he offered the sentence, "He hasn't been well from long time now, and I never know how to reach him."
He said that my dad came in and out of the house once in a blue moon, when he needed something, and never with heads up.
I figured he either didn't want to talk shit about his son, or that he didn't know that I already knew about the drugs, and didn't want to pile onto my plate. Whichever one it was, I decided against letting him know that I already knew, or had been warned by my mentor, rather, about both his and my uncle's early love affair with drugs.

My uncle, on the other hand, still lived there, and actually walked through the door while I was sitting at the table. Though one look at his sunken jaw-line and frail frame made it painfully apparent that he was indeed strung out, you could still see by the

● ● ●

way he stood tall with his shoulders back
that at some point in his life, he was way
more than what he had become. He looked
like my dad, too.

"Wow," Was all he repeated for the first few
minutes upon looking at me, while
simultaneously rubbing his head, bashfully.
"You... you're beautiful," He finally
managed.

I don't know exactly why, but I shifted
uncomfortably in my seat. I didn't want to
judge him just because he was on drugs. I
understood that everyone has a story and he
for sure had his, as did my father, but... I
don't know. I guess I just didn't know what
to expect. Know what I mean? So many
thoughts swarmed my mind at once:

*Is he high right now? Is he just coming
down from a high? Do drugs make him react
aggressively to things? Is he calling me
"beautiful" in the way that a man who's
tryna holla at a woman does? And if so...
ew? Does he not realize I'm his niece?
Maybe my grandfather didn't give him the
heads up. Maybe I'm on the verge of a
fucking panic attack because I'm just over-
fucking-thinking and need to chill the fuck
out, and breathe.*

I think that he picked up on my vibe, "No, I mean, yes. Yes you're beautiful, but… but… it's 'cause you look like mom."

Those words soothed me *right away*.

It was the third time for the day that I was staring into faces who not only shared my skin colour and facial features, but who were confirming that I was a part of them without a shadow of a doubt. Man…
All of the years I spent staring at myself in the mirror wondering, imagining, sad, crying; and now, here I was. I had found all of the missing pieces to my internal puzzle.

I left my grandfather's house that day feeling a sense of both peace and empowerment like I had never felt before. Though I never did get to actually meet my dad, it didn't matter. I had what I'd been searching for—knowledge.
All of these years, I just wanted to *know*. Like, damn. I just wanted to fucking know!

My grandfather and I promised to keep in touch, and we did for a little while. But, eventually, the contact faded, and to be honest, I'm not upset at that. My goal at thirty-one years old was not to go looking for this other half of me so that I could build relationships on that side. I know that may sound odd to some, but it's the truth. I mean, if it happened then it happened, and I wouldn't dismiss it, but that wasn't the goal. All I ever wanted… *was to know.*

So now what? I had gone back and dug up the roots of my issues and also found a part of myself that I had been questioning my entire fucking life, and was holding it all in my bare hands. For a little while, I found my brain looping this one sentence, *"Man… if only I had known then what I know now."* But I had to snap out of it.

What happened, happened.

I could not change the past so there was actually no use in stewing in it. Instead, I decided to sort through it and make a list of pros and cons.
The pros would be things about myself and mannerisms that I had taken on as a result of my childhood, that turned out to be great and aided me during the course of my life thus far.
The cons would be things about myself and mannerisms that I had taken on as a result of my childhood, that were crippling certain areas of my life thus far; things that I needed to *unlearn* and *get the entire fuck rid of.*

Pros:

My independence.
My creativity.
My survival instincts.
My ability to motivate myself.
My determination.
My ambition.
My empathy levels.
My compassion levels.
My heart.

Cons:

Allowing people (both men *and* women,
alike) to mistreat, and walk all over me.
Being afraid to use my voice.
Being afraid to stand up for myself.
Putting men on pedestals.
Doing what other people wanted me to do as
opposed to what I wanted to do.
Not creating, and enforcing clear
boundaries.
Staying in one-sided, toxic as fuck
relationships (friendships included.)

Once my list was in front of my face, it was
both settling and unsettling at the same
time.

Unsettling because, well… the cons. Like, gawt damn!

Settling because at least my pros were pretty fucking awesome, and those were what I was going to use as my foundation to build my self-love journey on.

As hard as going back to dig up my roots was, I'm glad I did it. As a matter of fact, I'm proud of myself for doing it.

No, I may not have been born into the most "ideal" of circumstances, and yes, clearly growing up I had a lot of issues and battles to fight that ended up following me into my adulthood as a result. But my journey back to the past gave me a sense of gratitude that I had never felt before. Shit could have been way worse for me, you know?

I, Cici, could have turned out *waaaaay* worse, and my list of pros help to show me that. So… now what?

For me, it all boiled down to two options:

A- I carried on living my life exactly how I had always lived it, expecting different results, while simultaneously blaming everything I did on what I lacked during my childhood.

B- Get to fucking work unlearning all of the unhealthy patterns I had already fallen into, and practice replacing them with patterns that would benefit my future and those who were going to be a part of that future.

I chose the latter.

I mean, come on! Yes, I definitely knew that I would have my work cut out for me and that it wasn't going to be easy at all; but so what? Nothing worth having comes easy, and for fuck's sake... it was time for me to realize that I, Cici, was fucking worth it. I was worth peace, healthy love, and true happiness. Yes I was!
I wanted to experience and maintain a mentally and emotionally *healthy* life for myself. I wanted to experience and maintain *healthy relationships* with men, too. Furthermore, I knew that I wanted to have children someday, and I did *not* want my children to have a mother who still had unresolved fucking daddy issues. A mother who practiced the blame game more than she practiced self-reflection and finding solutions. **And I did not want my children to have a mother who was lacking self-love.** How the hell would I be able to teach them things that I hadn't learned for myself? Nah. There was no way I was going to repeat my family history. Knowledge is power; and knowing what I knew, I had the

power to change the direction of where my life was headed... *for the better.*

Unapologetic:
Eviction and Boundary Notices

I didn't come to all of my realizations and just start cutting toxic people out of my life without warning—no. I still loved these people, after all, and most of them had been a part of my life, well… my whole damn life. My hope was that by them seeing a change in me, it would inspire them to change, too; that was both wrong and right of me, though. Right because my heart was in a good place, *"Let's all rise, together. Let's all help and support each other. Let's learn a new way together."* But it was wrong because you can't change people who don't see anything wrong with their actions/behaviours, and you can't change people who don't want to change for themselves.

Though I was finally able to identify and admit that these people were in fact toxic, I still was not prepared for the shitshow that was to come as a result of me working on my cons list. Start speaking up for yourself, doing what you want to do instead of what others want you to do, and putting boundaries in place for your own self-care, and watch how quickly those who were accustomed to walking all over you and abusing you begin to *lose their actual shit*. To say witnessing that shit up close and personal was disheartening would be an

understatement—it was straight up muthafucking heartbreaking.
Like, damn… I really was just around to be your punching bags, your "yes woman", your ego boosts, the mat you wiped your dirty fucking shoes on.
WooooooooOOOOW. Fucking, wow. Okay. Got it. I see you all crystal clear now.

Crystal. Fucking. Clear.

Alas, the meat of my self-love journey. Here I thought that I had completed the hard part by digging up my roots. Ha! No. *This shit* was the hard part. This was my test. This was where I had to prove to the Universe and God that I really wanted what I said I wanted: A better me and a better future; and guess what? You cannot better yourself around people who are committed to keeping you exactly the way you are.

• • •

What My Love for Myself Looks Like

I am a proud woman of colour.

I am an individual. A free spirit.
A risk-taker. An independent thinker.
A go-getter. A hustler. A rebel with a cause.
An ambivert. A creator. A lover. A giver.
I am a fucking survivor.

I am passionate. Romantic. Affectionate.
Sensitive. Gentle. Seductive. Graceful.
Assertive. Strong-willed. Bold. Considerate.
Compassionate. Vulnerable.
I have a voice. I have opinions. I love hard.
I blush easily. I laugh a lot.
I am flawed. I am stubborn. I am sarcastic.
I can absolutely be a brat sometimes.

I am a daughter. A granddaughter. A sister.
A niece. An aunty. A best friend to others,
and now... *A best friend to myself, too.*

I have learned to embrace and love my
entire journey thus far—the good *and* the
bad, and all of the things about me that make
me... *me.*

As I continue to unlock, meet, and shape
new parts of myself, I understand that self-
love stuff is not a joke, nor is it a hit and run.
Self-love is a lifelong commitment, and as I
evolve and move through new life

experiences, I see that with new levels come new devils, which means that I will always have to re-adjust my self-love levels in order to rise above whatever bullshit is thrown my way. My journey thus far has proven that there is nothing that I cannot create for myself so long as I am willing to put in the work, and no matter what happens along the way, I always have the power to switch gears when I want to… *because the key to my future is always around my own neck.*

I set the tone for how I want to be treated now. I value my mental and emotional health more than ever now.
The boundaries that I have put in place have proven to be one of the best things I could have ever done for myself, and these boundaries are *non-negotiable*, and apply to both *men and women*, alike.
No, you cannot be around me if you practice abuse.
No, you cannot be around me if you have a problem with me formulating my own opinions.
No, you cannot be around me if you are a bully.
No, you cannot be around me if you are only interested in taking the good from me, but never giving back.

• • •

No, you cannot be around me if you operate from a place of jealousy.

No, you cannot be around me if you are in competition with me.

No, you cannot be around me if you are in the habit of projecting your own insecurities onto others.

No, you cannot be around me if you're only okay with me doing good, so long as you feel like it's not "better" than you.

No, you cannot be around me if when a problem or misunderstanding arises, you are not interested in communicating in a RESPECTFUL manner, period.

I have been building a sanctuary for myself and it is filled with all of the things and people that contribute to my happiness, comfort, security, laughter, peace of mind, support, prayers and encouragement—if you cannot contribute to those very specific things, that's okay. I understand now that people can only give others what they have in them to give. It's okay to be exactly where you are in your own life, I am not here to force anyone to be anything for me that they aren't capable of being for themselves; but you can't stay around me… and *I am not sorry.*

I stopped apologizing for not wanting to be around people who attack both my personal growth and happiness, and threaten my desire to continue growing and being happy. I am not the broken woman that I used to be, therefore, I do not tolerate the same shit I used to.

Finally, *I have learned to love myself.*

Part 2:

My Ten Dating Commandments

One day, not too long after I made my list of "Pro's and Con's", I decided to also make a list of things I needed to change about the way I dated. This list slowly morphed into a guideline of dating reminders which I ended up calling *my dating commandments* as a joke, but actually, they've turned out to be something I've taken pretty seriously because they've helped me *a lot*...

*"I had this habit of always giving men
the benefit of the doubt,
which by itself wasn't a bad thing.
It became a bad thing when I began
completely closing my eyes to the bullshit."*

Commandment #1

Thou shalt not ignore red flags.

I look back at all of the most toxic relationships I have been in, in my twenties, and I can see *very clearly* that a lot of them happened because, well... I sucked at self-love, yes, we've established that in part one, but *also*, because I ignored the entire fuck out of red flags during the dating phase.

I'll give you a perfect example:

If you've read my first book, Letters to My Ex, then you will be very familiar with James. (If you haven't read my first book, well, girlfriend... get on that!) James was an actual billboard of red flags when we first began dating, and not only did I overlook them, I made excuses for them all.

Red Flag #1: He was money hungry, but not in a healthy way.

James was a schemer, basically. Anything he could do to put money in his pocket, he'd do, even if that meant lying to and/or manipulating people; and by people, I mean mostly women.

• • •

When he and I started dating, he was living with his mother. He'd explained to me that he'd moved out many times before, but never on his own. Basically, whenever he would leave his mother's house it would be to go live with a woman who already had her own place. It was only *after* he moved in with *me* that I began to realize this scheme of his. Moving in with women who already had their own places made it easy for him not to have to contribute very much to the house, because he knew that they would have to pay their shit, regardless. Feel me? Therefore, he could do the bare minimum and get away with it (i.e. Buy groceries and that's it.) This way, he got to go to work and literally save every dime he made.

Another thing I found out during our dating phase was that his car note was being paid by this chick who he swore up and down that he wasn't sleeping with.
The thing is, I remember hearing the actual sound of alarms going off in my fucking gut, like, "ATTENTION. ATTENTION. STEP AWAY FROM THIS GUY AND RUN IN THE OPPOSITE DIRECTION, IMMEDIATELY." But, instead of listening to those alarms, my ass gobbled up the fucking bullshit story he fed me about the situation. It wasn't until well after he'd

already moved in with me that I found out that he was, in fact, sleeping with her from time-to-time and toying with her mind and emotions. She was madly in love with him, and he was promising to be with her "when the time was right".

Red Flag #2: He got his ex pregnant.

Granted, this flag was presented well into our relationship, but it was a *serious* flag, nonetheless. Considering the fact that he and I were no longer using protection, not only did he get another woman pregnant, but he was also putting my health at risk by sleeping with her and god knows WHO else unprotected, too? Nah, man. Fucking, no.

RED FUCKING FLAG, SIS.

But, again, my ass fell for the story he gave me and the promises he made to me… and I stayed. I stayed with a man who had a baby with someone else on the way.

Red Flag #3: *All* of my friends hated him.

Yes, it's your life, and you can do whatever you want, and your friends opinions shouldn't be the determining factor in your decisions. However… when every single one of your *truest* friends are like:

"Girl, no."
"Seriously? *Nooooo.*"
"This guy is trouble with a capital T. What the actual fuck are you doing?"
"Do I need to smack some sense into you, or…?"

That shit should speak *volumes.*

Unfortunately, at the time my self-love levels were hella low, and even though, deep down, I knew my friends were right, my thirst for love and affection from a man overpowered all logic.
This is why it's so important to learn how to fucking love yourself before you throw yourself into relationships with men.
This. Is. Fucking. Why.

Red Flag #4: He wanted to isolate me.

On the flip side, James hated all of my friends too; obviously, because they were constantly trying to get me the hell out of that relationship.

● ● ●

Piece of shit boyfriends don't like their girlfriends having honest and real best friends, because they want to keep being pieces of shit in peace.

So, what did he do? He was in my ear, daily, telling me that they were all just jealous that I had a man and they didn't. He'd often say that they wished they could have someone to go home to at the end of the night, and that they wanted to break up my relationship because (and I quote directly from his mouth), "Misery loves company. None of them can keep a man so they don't want to see you with one." *Gag.*

Hindsight is always 20/20, man.
Of course all of my friends wanted to have what I had! Who wouldn't be jealous of a girl who's in a relationship with a guy who had a baby on the way by another woman, stuck his dick in every chick in town behind her back, lived in her house and barely paid for a goddamn thing, fought with her all the time, disrespected the fuck out of her all the time, and had a serious habit of shitting on and belittling her dreams? Come on!
THAT IS THE EXACT TYPE OF MAN THAT EVERY WOMAN PRAYS FOR.......... *not*. Fucking, not!

• • •

Red flags are real, and now when they show up—I trust them.

*"My purpose in life isn't to sit around
waiting or begging
for someone to treat me right."*

Commandment #2

Thou shalt not beg for anything that should be an automatic given.

I look around, and it pains me to see that so many of us women have either had, or are currently experiencing the same storylines.

Being treated like shit by a man while begging for him to do better and give us the minimal love, affection, and respect has been the direct source of many of our tears, sleepless nights, stress and heartache. They say that when you're truly fed up— and I mean *truly* fed up and not merely repeatedly telling yourself that you're fed up—you'll take action. Well, one day I woke up and took action.

I'm a pretty simple chick. I'm not hard to please or get smiling *at all*. Interestingly enough, I realized that **the only men I've ever dated who have ever pegged me as "complicated" or "too much", are the ones who wanted me to give them one hundred percent without them having to give me the same in return.** Fuck you, bro. I shouldn't have to ask or, worse, *beg* someone to reciprocate the respect I give to them, or to *not* do to me what they wouldn't want done to them. Especially in the dating stages. Like, what the actual fuck? Enough of the bullshit already. You will either see me as your equal and treat me as such, or you can get to fucking steppin' all the way out of my life.

*"I'm never going to be the woman
that they want me to be.*

*I'm always going to be the woman
that I want to be."*

Commandment #3

Thou shalt not change all of the things you love about yourself, just to make someone else happy.

Listen, Linda. *Listen.*

I've learned that there's a very big difference between changing things about yourself because they are having a massively negative impact on those you come in contact with, and changing things about yourself that are just fucking fine simply because someone else wants you to be who they want you to be.
Big. Fucking. Difference. Okay? Example:

I'm a very free-spirited, bubbly, fun-loving person. I'm the type who will start dancing and singing along to the music playing in the clothing store without a care in the world. I'm the type who will get in the cart at the grocery store and be like, "Push me", just for fun! I shriek when I'm genuinely excited about something. When something is funny, I burst into a fit of laughter.

None of those things are hurting anyone;
they are not character flaws.

Yet, for a long time, I found myself
believing that they *were* character flaws due
to a relationship I was in. The man I was
dating at the time apparently hated all of
those free-spirited, fun-loving traits that
made me who I was, and had been vocal
about his dislike of them a few months into
us dating. He was very reserved in public,
and would often tell me that I was
embarrassing him, or that I needed to "tone
it down". *"Why must you always be so "on"*
all of the time? Relax. Learn how to contain
yourself. You don't have to start dancing in
the middle of the store. You don't have to
shriek when you're excited, causing
everyone to look at you. Seriously, learn
how to relax and contain your emotions. It's
embarrassing."

I didn't want him to be embarrassed by me, I
wanted him to be proud of me, so I stopped
doing the things that made me, me. I let him
tell me who he wanted me to be, and I
became that. The result? I was constantly
walking on eggshells around him. I was
never sure what I should or shouldn't say or
do, so I pretty much only spoke when
spoken to and followed his lead to a fault.

I was fucking miserable. I so badly missed who I naturally was, but kept working to "contain" those parts of myself, instead. What kind of a life was that? A sad one, that's what kind. But I've since forgiven myself for that shit.

Today, my self-love levels are so high that there's no fucking way I'm letting anyone try to change parts of me to better suit them.

Get the *fuck* outta here.

Everyone ain't for everyone, and that's okay! Now I tell men all the time, "Go find a woman who already comes with the traits you enjoy." End of story.

"The game changer, for me?
Well, amongst other things,
I started to treat my
romantic relationships with men,
the same way I treated my relationships
with my homegirls.
Basically, if I wouldn't tolerate
my homegirls disrespecting me
time after time again,
then I wasn't about to take it
from no man, either."

Commandment # 4

Thou shalt not tolerate from a man, anything you wouldn't tolerate from a friend.

I remember when I started to think about the shit I put up with from men, compared to the shit I would *never* put up with from my friends. I felt sick. The pedestal that I put the men in my life on was *absolutely sickening.* Then I thought about some of the friends I had who did the exact same thing when it came to men, and it truly opened my eyes.

At some point or another, we had all had boyfriends who had no jobs and lived with us rent free, used our cars every day but had no money to fill the tank back up, and got tickets on our cars that they never payed. Bro, what? Oh, and the icing on the cake? They'd throw us under the bus whenever they were around other women, or shit on our dreams whenever we mustered the courage to be vocal about them. They'd say shit to us like, "Without me, you're nothing." Hold up. *Excuse the actual fuck outta me, sir?*

Yet, there was no way in *hell* that *any of us* would take that level of shit from each other. What do you mean you're squatting in my house for a year, heffa? Taking my car whenever you please and not putting gas back in it, etc... ? It would be simple: "Listen, girlfriend. You ain't gotta go home, but you've gotta get the fuck up outta here." How sad, though. What the fuck were we doing? Seriously? Nah, man. NO. I was done living like that and put into my brain that the only difference between the relationships between my friends and any man in my life was sex and physical affection; and I was done letting those two things be the excuse for tolerating piss poor behaviour. Fuck that. I began putting everyone in my life that I loved on the same *equal* playing level.

*"It was probably around
4:30AM when I called her,
waking her out of her sleep.
I was crying so hard
that I could barely fucking talk.
You know the type of crying that you do
when you're hurting badly,
but from the inside?
Yeah. It was that kind.
All I could manage to tell her was,
"I need you right now."
She didn't ask why.
She didn't even ask what happened.
The only thing she asked was for my location.
In less than twenty minutes
she walked through my front door in her PJ's
and a headscarf wrapped around her hair.
Do you know who she was?*

My best fucking friend."

Commandment # 5

Thou shalt not forget about your friends just because a new man has entered your life.

Getting to know someone new is fun and exciting. You just wanna be around them every chance you get.

One of the things I used to do was completely push my homegirls to the side whenever a new man came along; and that was horrible of me. Now I am able to see that this too was a direct result of my daddy issues. I'm sure we all know the saying, *"Men will come and go, but your friends are for a lifetime",* and while as we grow older we learn that friends are definitely not exempt from leaving your life either, the premise of the saying holds a lot of weight for me, personally. My homegirls cannot be used just to help me pick up the pieces of my broken heart, then shelved when I am back in the swing of things, floating on cloud nine with a new man until he fucks up. **That's not fucking cool, and it's not fucking fair.**

To my homegirls who've I done this to, who I know are reading this right now, I know that I've apologized a thousand times for that shit already, but… one more time… I'm fucking sorry. Thank y'all for still being here, by my side.

"I wasn't upset at anyone.

There wasn't any anger in my heart, either.
My decision to be alone was just that—
my decision.

I had spent my life taking care of others;
making sure they were okay and feeling loved,
and as much as it was heavy for me, many times,
and even though some people took advantage
of my loving hands and heart,
I was happy that I could be there for those
when they were in need.
But it was my turn to take care of myself,
and I wanted to feed myself in all
departments—
mentally, spiritually, emotionally, creatively.
I wanted to challenge myself.
I wanted to blossom.

I thought about my career dreams and goals,
and I wanted to focus on and nurture them
without having to compromise with anyone else.
I thought about the love affair I had
with sun-kissed sandy beaches
and beautiful blue waters,
and I wanted to be able to run to them
whenever my heart desired, and stay with them
for as long as my bank account said I could,
without feeling like I had to consider
someone else before packing my suitcases.

While many people around me
were settling down, or turning up pregnant,

*I was longing for something that seemed
like only I understood—freedom.
Freedom to get to know myself better.
Freedom to come and go as I pleased.
Freedom to spend the money I earned
however I wanted to.
Freedom to close my eyes, stretch my wings,
and let the wind push me to places that I knew
didn't only exist in my dreams.*

*I had let people in,
and shared my world with them
so many times before, selflessly and willingly.*

But this time...

I wanted to experience my world by myself.

Selfishly, and unapologetically."

Commandment # 6

Thou shalt not forget about yourself just because a new man has entered your life.

Here's what I've learned about dating:
It's not a fucking committed relationship.

I didn't embrace the true meaning of dating until my late twenties. Society likes to tell women that if you're dating a guy, then that's it—it can *only* be him. Meanwhile, society tells men to play the field. Test different women out. *Find what they like.* No wonder why the majority of men that I knew weren't ever stressing over one woman; they kept their options open until they truly found the one that grabbed their hearts! I was doing it all wrong. This is part of the reason why, today, I'm so anti-rules when it comes to society's standards. Half of these piece of shit rules geared towards women were put into place by a patriarchy, and once I understood that, oh…
I was done.

Don't get me wrong here, this wasn't just a, "If men can do it, I can do it, too," moment.

No. It was much more than that.

This was an observation that turned into a study, that turned into an experiment, that turned into me living my actual best fucking life and finally *enjoying men* as opposed to wanting to punch them all in their throats.

Learning how to date men without feeling the need to immediately cling to them and put all of my eggs into one basket was incredibly *liberating*, and *empowering*. It taught me how to *put myself first*, and not compromise the things *I* still wanted to do for what someone else didn't want me to do, thus leading me to also give men the freedom of choice:

*"This is who I am. This is where I'm currently at in my life. These are the things I'd like to achieve for **myself** moving forward, with or without someone in my life in any capacity. I am a spur of the moment type of woman. There are places I plan on travelling to at any given moment, for an undecided period of time, with or without company; and I've worked hard to build the type of career that can allow me the freedom to do that. Right now, I am not interested in slowing down or stopping anything that I am doing, or want to do, simply because you*

● ● ●

and I are "talking" "sleeping together"
"getting to know each other", etc.
I completely understand if these are things
you don't see yourself being able to handle.
You are allowed to feel how you feel, want
what you want, and be with someone who
will compliment your current lifestyle and/or
space that you are in. I'm not interested in
forcing you to stay, nor am I saying you
*have to leave. **The choice is entirely yours.***
But this is where I stand. Take it or leave
it."

Now, this doesn't mean that I am anti-
commitment, by the way. I believe *healthy*
commitments are beautiful. I also believe
that a commitment between two people is
just that—it's between those two people.
Which means, the terms of one couples'
commitment to each other may not be the
same kind of terms I would agree to, and
vice versa. One size does not fit all, and
that's okay. For myself, however, everything
has to be organic.

Any man I date has to fit into my world,
seamlessly, and if he has plans on being my
actual boyfriend, then he has to know that
there are some things I won't be sacrificing
or leaving behind just because I'm

127

committing to him—like my *freedom* and my *individuality*.

No, I won't be entertaining other men if we've agreed to be exclusive, duh; that's not what I mean by "freedom". What I mean is that I will always need *my own space* every now and then. It could be a trip out of town alone. A long drive by myself. Perhaps a night in a hotel suite with a good book, my laptop, a bottle of my favorite champagne and a side of strawberries *just* for me.

I am, after all, an ambivert and a writer; I will always need that space alone to recharge, think, reminisce, dream and create. I am my own person, *my own woman*; and now that I have gotten to know myself, completely, and have embraced *me*…

I'm not leaving myself behind for anyone.

Any man who wants to be with me, on any level, will not only have to truly understand all of that, but will also have to be secure enough within himself to understand that it has absolutely nothing to do with him, and everything to do with me.

*"There's nothing sexier to me
than an ambitious, go-getting man,
who loves the fact that I am an equally
ambitious, go-getting woman."*

Commandment #7

Thou shalt not entertain any man who doesn't have any ambitions of his own, or who has a problem with yours.

By now, it's no secret that I am an insanely ambitious woman. I've never been the type to wait for shit to magically happen for me, or wait on a man with money to take care of me and pay my way through this world. No thanks. He who giveth, can taketh right the fuck back from you. I've worked my ass off for everything that I've ever had, and continue to do so.

I've been a hustler since I was twelve years old (give or take). From braiding hair on the stoop and charging five bucks a head, to shoveling people's stairs and walkways in the winter, charging ten bucks per house, to being the block babysitter, charging twenty bucks per kid—I have always loved earning my own money, and my ambition has always been sky-fucking-high. There is no limit for me, hence why I have never been a 9-to-5 type of woman. I have never liked the idea of feeling like there was a ceiling above me, limiting me to a "fixed" amount of income, or working to build someone else's shit, or being grounded to a specific building, or working on someone else's schedule.

I'm not shitting on anyone who works a 9-to-5, by the way—chill. I'm just saying that it isn't, and never was for me.

I am a true entrepreneur, through and through; and just like a 9-to-5 isn't for me, being an entrepreneur isn't for everyone, either. Believe that!
I love the grind. I love both the highs and lows, equally. The risks that come along with it keeps me humble, hungry and always on my toes. This is a major part of why the whole "boyfriend" thing gets tricky for me. A lot of men I've come across and/or dated either:

• Don't understand me.

• Pretend they understand me but actually don't.

• Are hella ambitious and also extremely well off financially, and want me to be a housewife in exchange for them paying for everything.

• Have major issues with how much I work and complain about it every other week.

• Feel some type of way when they realize I make more money than them.

• Have zero ambition of their own and think that they can live off of me.

It's like, YO! I don't have time for *any* of that shit. You're either going to respect, support, encourage, love and *be proud* of THE FUCKING BOSS that I am, or leave me the entire fuck alone.

*"I've put myself on a backburner
one too many times over a man.
Call me what you want to,
but I'm not doing that shit to myself
ever-fucking-again."*

Commandment # 8

Thou shalt not ever allow a heartbreak to stop you from getting your coins.

Whenever I talk about dating versus a committed relationship, for some reason, there are a plethora of people who immediately assume that because I'm only dating, then I'm somehow magically immune from getting my heart broken. Bruh… stop this.

Developing feelings, feeling an attachment, *falling in love* is not only reserved for fucking commitments. Like, hello? You spend enough time with a person that you're into and enjoy, and yes… feelings, in some capacity, are bound to form.
It's called being a human-fucking-being.

Another thought process that many people seem to be married to, is that heartbreaks can only occur due to cheating, being lied to, betrayal, a toxic relationship—literally anything that has a grand drama associated with it. Why? Ever consider that your heart can break simply because something has run its natural course? Ever consider that your heart can break because you have to cut ties with someone for *their* own good, because you know that *you're* not in the position to give them what they need and you don't want to drag them along, selfishly? Damn.

A heartbreak doesn't only happen as a result of a tsunami, and my thing is:
No matter how badly my heart is hurting due to a situation with a man, I cannot allow it to slow down my hustle. I have to get up, get moving, and go get my coins.
As cold as this is going to sound, the fact is—LIFE GOES ON.

Doesn't mean that I won't still care about that man. Doesn't mean that I will stop thinking about him, or even perhaps hoping/wanting things to work themselves out, eventually. It simply means that man is not responsible for getting my bag… I AM. Feel me?

Beyond my lights needing to be kept on, food needing to put in my fridge, clothes needing to be put on my back and a roof needing to be kept over my head, I have *real life dreams* that I need to keep a solid grip on if I ever want to see them manifest into realities. As the saying goes, *"Dreams don't work unless you do,"* and I will be fucking

damned if I let a heartbreak over a man be
the reason that I stop working to achieve my
dreams.

"You can't expect to have all of these good things and people, waltz into your life if you have a negative ass frame of mind."

Commandment # 9

Thou shalt not refer to all men as trash.

The "all men are trash" statement is legitimately starting to sound like nails on a chalkboard to me.

I have friends who swear by that statement, there are a million memes/quotes on social media that endorse that statement; and don't get me wrong—*I get it.* Get fucked over enough times by men and combine that with hearing so many other women's stories about getting fucked over by men, and yes… there is a strong disdain that begins to develop.

I had a period of my own when that was my frame of mind, too. Admittedly, it was a time when I was ridiculously bitter. I'm talking, I would see couples on the street holding hands and think to myself, "Awe, how cute. Enjoy that while it lasts, sis, because HE'S PROBABLY JUST USING YOU FOR WHATEVER HE CAN GET OUTTA YOU, THEN HE'S GOING TO STOMP ALL OVER YOUR HEART WITH NO REMORSE," type bitter.

Not my finest period in life, thank you very much. *Whew!*

But after a while of living with that frame of mind, while having the audacity to try to date at the same time and failing miserably, it dawned on me that I was hands-down sabotaging myself. Obviously I was failing miserably at dating, I was a breath of negative ass air—duh! Since when does having an overwhelmingly shitty attitude ever deliver overwhelmingly positive results?

I'll wait. *Mmmhhhmm.*

If I was always grouping ALL men into one category, then what was I honestly expecting the results to be? I was literally on some, "All men are trash," in one breath, then, "Where are all the good men at?" in the next. I mean, does that not sound a tad bit counter-fucking-productive to anyone else, or...?
To add to that, in general, how many good people do you know that jump at the chance to be around negative people? No, seriously. When's the last time you heard a good person say, "Man, I just love people who take the shit that they've been through with other people out on me! Now that's the type

of energy I want to be around everyday. Sign me up!" Yeah... my bet is not that fucking many.

If you are familiar with my work, you will know that I have a lot of, "I had to get real with myself," moments. Well, here comes another one:

I, as a woman, certainly am not, nor have I ever been interested in being in the company of a man who is so jaded by his previous experiences with women, that he projects that shit onto every other woman he meets because in his mind, *we're all the same.* Therefore, where did I get off thinking that any man would want to be around my stank attitude havin', projecting onto him, ass? Feel me?

And listen, man. Again, *I get it!* Shit is hard when you've been trampled over more times than you care to elaborate on; but for me, at some point, logic had to come before my feelings. (And I'm a fucking Pisces, okay? I eat, sleep, breathe and drool in my damn feelings. Smh. Emotional ass. So *trust me* when I say, *I know* it isn't easy). The facts are, whether you believe it or not, dope ass men with dope ass hearts exist too, and once I changed my attitude and also started practicing self-love, that's when I began to experience them for myself. It was, and still very much is *absolutely fucking beautiful.* That turning point was everything, and not only was I able to finally enjoy men, but I was also able to *accept* that just because you find a man that *is* a great man and he connects with you on a deeper level, that does not mean that he is meant to be *your* man. Circumstances and timing are both very real things, and they need to be treated as such. I think this is where a lot of us women get the lines blurred, and can also be quite the little hypocrites. Before you get in your feelings about that last sentence and start feeling personally attacked, let me explain…

I've had amazing men come into my life, and we've vibed together on a seriously *magical* level, but the circumstances and/or timing for a committed relationship weren't right. I can give you two perfect examples of this: The first comes right out of my second book, Blush. (Which, again, if you haven't read that book, either, you really need to stop sleeping on yo girl!)
Nathan was actually the man of my dreams, and damn near every other woman's dreams who knew him, or read the book; but the timing wasn't right for me. As beautiful of a

man as Nathan was, inside and out, and as much as he wanted us to be "official", I had just gotten out of a relationship not too long before meeting him, and simply wasn't in a place where I wanted to be someone's girlfriend again. I wanted to stand on my own two feet for a while, get to know myself further, and do me.

Now, does the fact that I didn't want to be with him in the way that he wanted to be with me make me a heartless bitch? A narcissist? A piece of shit? Someone who played games with his heart? *Trash*? Muthafucking, NO.

He and I got very close as we were dating, and we spent a lot of time together. All of my friends loved him, all of his friends loved me. We treated each other with respect, appreciation, and poured insane amounts affection onto each other. Yes, he was hurt when I declined his proposal to level up our relationship and go from just dating to committed, but I wasn't the one who hurt him—*the circumstances and timing are what hurt.* Big difference!

I didn't string Nathan along, and I never lied to him. Everything was mutual, until it wasn't. He wasn't wrong for wanting more from me, from *us*, than he had anticipated ever wanting in the beginning, and I wasn't

• • •

wrong for *not* wanting more than what we had.

Now, here's what I mean when I speak about us being little hypocrites sometimes:

Every woman who knows what went down between Nathan and I, including those who got to read all about it through the book, applauded me for staying true to *myself* and doing what was *best for me*. But enter example number two...

Same exact situation, but in reverse. I met someone years later—Anthony. We were dating. Shit was clear, and mutual. I never intended to fall for Anthony as hard as I did, but it happened. Months into us dating and falling into somewhat of a routine together, I found myself wanting to be with him on another level. One day, over a wonderful lunch date, I decided that it was time I confessed to him how I was feeling... so, I did just that.

Now, Anthony was/is extremely introverted and sensitive. Whenever he is caught off guard with any information, he likes to process it deeply before he reacts. Of course, my confession caught him all the way off guard, and because I knew him that well, I told him that he didn't have to answer me right away and that he could take his time. Two days later, in the early morning, I received a very long, thought out, respectful and gentle as fuck text message from him explaining in detail why he was not in the position to move forward with me the way I wanted to move forward with him.

Hello? I was *crushed*.
I definitely felt rejected. I definitely felt like shit. I definitely cried my eyes out for a good two weeks. When I told my girls what had happened, IMMEDIATELY, I was hit with, "Fuck him, B! You deserve better."

"What a piece of shit, honestly. Why would he drag you along if he never intended on being with you?"

"How dare he? Doesn't he know what kind of a DOPE ass woman he has in front of him?"

"Nah, Fam. He's trash. Next!"

I was like, "Okay, so let me get this straight. When it was me not wanting to be with Nathan under the *same exact circumstances*, that was all good; but now the situation is in reverse, and y'all are shitting on Anthony? The fuck?"

I was so irritated. Anthony was in no way, shape or form anything bad at all. Like, damn. A man can't treat you *well and properly* unless he's interested in committing to you? Y'all can't snuggle, watch movies, go to dinner, share affection, have deep life convo's, hold hands or sleep over at each other's houses UNLESS his intention is to commit to you? If he does any, or all of those things, and doesn't commit to you in the end, it means he was stringing you along? Playing games with you? Trash? Stop, man. Stop!

Yes, my feelings got hella hurt! But Anthony did not hurt me—*the circumstances and the timing did.*
Just like I was honest with Nathan about where I stood, Anthony was honest with me. You want to know what would have been wrong? If I continued on with Nathan, *knowing* he wanted more than I was able/willing to give, and if Anthony continued on with me, *knowing* I wanted more than he was able/willing to give—then we'd be flying into the stringing people along, piece of shit, and trash zone.

• • •

Not all men are trash; and holding onto that mentality would only prevent me from appreciating some extremely amazing men that came into my life, and being grateful for the experiences I had with them while we were on the same page.

"I got caught up for a moment,
and relapsed back into an old version of myself.

The girl who fought for people
who weren't fighting for her.
Cared too much for people
while they cared less about her.
Ignored her own intuition,
dismissing things that just weren't adding up.
The girl who stayed quiet
about things that were bothering her,
all because she didn't want
any possible conflict.

I got caught up for a moment,
and relapsed into an old version of myself...

but today, I put my foot down,
confronted that girl firmly and said,
"I'm sorry, sis, but you've gotta go."

Commandment #10

Thou shalt remind yourself of your worth.

Through my journey in life, self-love, dating and relationships, I've learned a lot. But two really important things that I work at keeping in mind are:

1- Relapses are a part of life.

Shit happens. We all fall off the wagon sometimes, there is no way around that. It just is what the fuck it is.

2- Dust yourself off, deep breath and carry on.

I am very hard on myself. Sometimes too hard, in fact. I used to do this thing where I'd forgive others easily for their mistakes and never hold grudges against them, but when it came to my own mistakes, I'd hold these absurd grudges against myself forever. Time after time again, every person in my life who has ever truly loved me have all said the same thing at some point, *"B...*

fucking relax. You are way too hard on yourself. Give yourself a break. You're only human."

You're only human—that part.

Yes, today I absolutely know my fucking worth, but I also know that certain circumstances, feelings, or moments in my life can push me right the fuck off of my worth-wagon; and guess what? That's okay.

Gawt damn it, that is OKAY. You know why? Because nothing is perfect, nothing is constant or guaranteed, and context is *everything*.
Every now and again I will fall and, depending on how quickly my wagon was moving, it might hurt a little, or it might hurt a lot. I might have a slight bruise, or I might end up with a cut so deep that it leaves a scar. Regardless, the goal is to forgive myself, get the fuck back up, and go hop back on MY wagon.

When it comes to dating and relationships, listen, man… unless my plan is to never interact with a man ever again—which is certainly not—*men are a part of life!* I'm going to meet some good ones, I'm going to meet some shitty ones. I'm going to meet some who *stay* good, just like I'm going to meet some that morph into actual piles of stinking shit after some time, leaving me completely stunned. I'm going to meet some who lie to me from the beginning, and I'm going to meet some who are going to tell me the truth—even if that truth isn't what I'm expecting—good or bad. Let's face it, not all truths are sweet.

I can be in a place in my life where I'm 1000% not interested in a committed relationship, and instead, only want to date and have fun, which is fine… *I'm allowed.* But I am in no way, shape or form, immune from meeting a man who opens my heart up so much, that it changes my mind and I end up wanting to be with him and *only him*; and just because I change my mind and take that leap, doesn't mean that it will work out the way that *I* want it to in that moment.

If you've read all of my books, starting with Letters to My Ex, my evolution as a woman (and a writer for that matter) is actually documented. My pen used to be filled with ink that was a special blend of angry, sad, hurt, disturbed and bitter, and I had so many questions, *"Why did he hurt me like this? How could he do this to me? Why is this happening to me again? Where is my self-*

worth? Why don't I love myself enough?"—
but that's just where I was in my life. I was a
walking, talking, living blend of that ink.
I published Letters to My Ex February 29th,
2015, but the letters that were inside of that
book were written over a course of three
years, after James and I had broken up,
which was when I was twenty-five years
old.

It is 2018, I am thirty-three years old as I
write this book, and I just don't have the
same type of ink in my pen anymore.
Everything about me has evolved, including
the way I think and the way I view men and
relationships with them, whether in the form
of friendships, dating, or a commitment.

I can be angry at a man for turning out to be
a fucktard, I can be angry for shit not going
the way I wanted it to go, and I can be angry
at myself—all that is natural. But what I've
learned that I absolutely cannot do anymore,
under any circumstances, is *stay* angry—not
at a man, not at a situation, and most
definitely not with myself. It's too heavy,
too draining, and it doesn't benefit me, or
any area of my life at-fucking-all.
What's meant for me will always be for me,
and I really began understanding that every
experience that I have, and whatever comes

• • •

from those experiences *are* meant for me—including my relapses and falling off of my wagon. Shit is going to happen, and I may very well lose sight of my worth from time to time while I'm involved with a man; what's important is that I don't let it *stay* lost. What's important is that the moment I realize that I'm out of tune with *myself,* I get a grip by reminding myself of who the fuck I am and what the fuck I *am* worth, dust myself off, take a deep breath and carry the fuck on with my life with a heart and soul that are *inspired,* as opposed to angry and bitter.

At the end of the day, I am a strong woman because I embrace all of my weak moments and learn from them, not because I don't ever have any or think that I am above or immune to them.

So, there you have it. Now you know how I learned to love myself and how I manage my dating life as a result. Maybe your self-love journey has been similar to mine, maybe it hasn't. Maybe you're going to try out my dating commandments for yourself, maybe they aren't your cup of Henny, so you won't. Maybe my dating commandments simply inspired you to write your own, for yourself. (Which, by the way, I totally encourage. Writing shit down helps; trust me, I've made a whole gawt damn career out it.) At the beginning of this book, I wrote, *"Everything becomes a lot easier once you love yourself... so I've learned"*—regardless of where you're at in your journey right now and which direction you decide to take from here, just remember that—it's bible.

XOX,

B

The

SELF-LOVE BIBLE

How I Learned to Love Myself

THE CRIMSON KISS

INSTAGRAM-FACEBOOK-TWITTER @THECRIMSONKISS

Previous books by Cici.B

Letters to My Ex
Blush
Lost and Found: The Book of Short Stories
Spilled Words: The Crimson Kiss Quote Collection
Girl Power: The Crimson Kiss Quote Collection II
12:02AM Volume 1: Exploring B

Made in the USA
Monee, IL
30 July 2020